Spot the Shape

Shapes in the Garden

Rebecca Rissman

Heinemann Library
Chicago, Illinois

W9-BRE-486

© 2009 Heinemann Library
an imprint of Capstone Global Library, LLC
Chicago, Illinois

Customer Service: 888-454-2279

Visit our website at www.heinemannraintree.com

Designed by Joanna Hinton-Malivoire
Photo research by Tracy Cummins and Heather Mauldin
Color Reproduction by Dot Gradations Ltd, UK
Printed in the United States of America in Stevens Point, Wisconsin.

062011
006273

Library of Congress Cataloging-in-Publication Data
Rissman, Rebecca.
Shapes in the garden / Rebecca Rissman.
p. cm. -- (Spot the shape!)
Includes bibliographical references and index.
ISBN 978-1-4329-2168-2 (hc) -- ISBN 978-1-4329-2174-3 (pb) 1. Shapes--Juvenile literature. I. Title.
QA445.5.R5727 2008
516'.15--dc22
                              2008043205

Acknowledgments
The author and publishers are grateful to the following for permission to reproduce copyright material: ©Alamy pp. **4** (G P Bowater), **6** (Philipp Zechner), **9** (Tom Mackie), **10** (Tom Mackie), **17** (Caro), **18** (Caro); ©Shutterstock pp. **11** (Bill Perry), **12** (Bill Perry), **13** (Salamanderman), **14** (Salamanderman), **15** (MaxPhoto), **16** (MaxPhoto), **19** (Kevin Eaves), **20** (Kevin Eaves), **21** (Salamanderman), **23** (Bill Perry); ©SuperStock pp. **7** (fStop), **8** (fStop).

Cover photograph of Chateau De Hautefort, France reproduced with permission of ©Alamy/ PCL. Back cover photograph of a garden shed reproduced with permission of ©SuperStock (fStop).

Every effort has been made to contact copyright holders of any material reproduced in this book. Any omissions will be rectified in subsequent printings if notice is given to the publisher.

Contents

Shapes 4

Shapes in Gardens. 6

Naming Shapes 22

Picture Glossary. 23

Index 24

Shapes

Shapes are all around us.

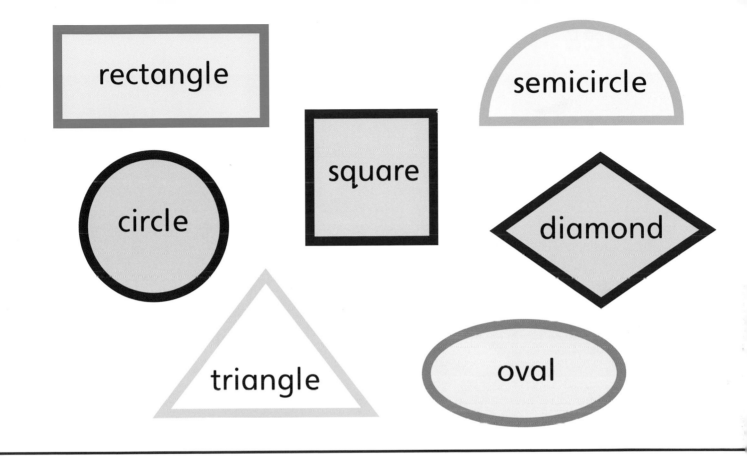

Each shape has a name.

Shapes in Gardens

There are many shapes in a garden.

What shape is this shed door?

This shed door is a rectangle.

What shape is this pond?

This pond is an oval.

What shape can you see under this bridge?

The shape under this bridge is
a semicircle.

What shape are these hedges?

These hedges are squares.

What shape can you see in
this flower?

There is a circle in this flower.

What shapes are in this fence?

There are diamonds in this fence.

What shape is this tree?

This tree is a triangle.

There are many shapes in this garden.
What shapes can you see?

Naming Shapes

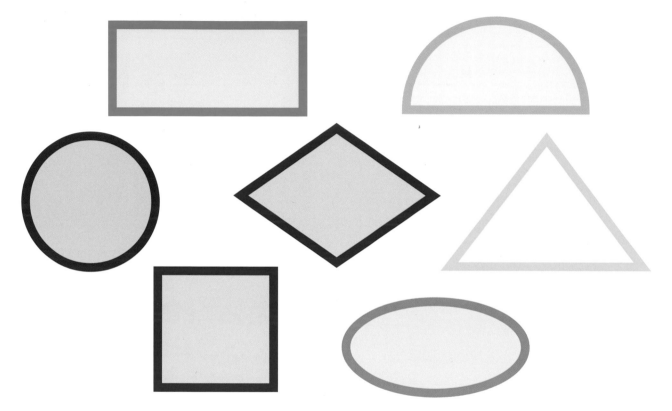

Can you remember the names of these shapes?

Picture Glossary

 **hedge** a line of bushes, trees, or shrubs planted close together

Index

circle 5, 16

diamond 5, 18

oval 5, 10

rectangle 5, 8

semicircle 5, 12

square 5, 14

triangle 5, 20

Note to Parents and Teachers
Before reading
Using cardstock, make two sets of the shapes shown on page 22. Give each child a shape and tell him or her to explore the room looking for things that are the same shape. Explain that shapes can be many different sizes.

After reading
Garden Collage: cut a variety of shapes from colored paper (for example, green triangles, brown rectangles and squares, yellow circles, purple diamonds, pink semicircles, and red ovals). Ask children to use the shapes to make flowers, trees, and bushes. Help them glue their shapes onto a piece of paper to make a garden collage.